FOINTAMA
A Play

Kelvin Ngong Toh

Langaa Research & Publishing CIG
Mankon, Bamenda

Publisher:
Langaa RPCIG
Langaa Research & Publishing Common Initiative Group
P.O. Box 902 Mankon
Bamenda
North West Region
Cameroon
Langaagrp@gmail.com
www.langaa-rpcig.net

Distributed in and outside N. America by African Books Collective
orders@africanbookscollective.com
www.africanbookcollective.com

ISBN: 9956-791-73-3

DISCLAIMER
All views expressed in this publication are those of the author and do not necessarily reflect the views of Langaa RPCIG.

Dedication

To

Mama Esther Nain Toh,

Justice Prudence Galega,

Dr. Eunice Ngong Kum,

Women of rigour and foresight.

Surely men of low degree are vapour,
Men of high degree are a lie
If they are weighed on the scales,
They are altogether *lighter* than vapour.
Psalm 62:9

Table of Content

Dramatis Personae

Fointama: Head of the Fon's Hunters

Princess of Fuli

Ayeah: Prince of Belo

Chief of Belo

Chief of Fuli

Bangsibu: Oracle

Tufoin and Yuh: Palace attendants at Fuli

Ngam: Boy

Ndum: Princess of Fuli's Maid

Bobe-Aboh: Executioner

Ngoh and Ntam: Hunters

Ajimsimbom, Abembom and Malayena: Village judges

Prologue

A Grove

Enter the priest.
He is old and dressed in ritual attire.
He takes two steps to the left side of his grove,
Makes some incantations,
Pours some libations,
Sings a song of appeasement and
Then, returns to his original position.
He sits down.

Enter Ngam, a young man.

Ngam
Is Bobe Mbangsibu in his shrine?
Ba, can you hear me?

Bangsibu
Yes son. Come in.
What is the news from the world of the living?

Ngam
Old one, the land is pregnant.

Bangsibu
Pregnant?

Ngam
Yes Ba. Pregnant

Bangsibu

Laughs and stretches his old limbs
When do you think the land will put to birth?

Ngam

The land?

Bangsibu

Yes. The land.

Ngam

Put to birth?

Bangsibu

Yes. Put to birth.

Ngam

Why?

Bangsibu

Because it is pregnant.

Ngam

What I mean is that there is an abomination in the land.
There is a snake on our roof and if we are not careful,
It will finish with us. In fact, the cock has laid an egg.
And it might produce an adder.

Bangsibu

You speak like an elder.
Your words are strong and indirect like those of your elders.
[Aside]
They have learned the cunning tongue to deal with the poor.
They use their indirect tongues to manipulate the poor.
They think their cunning tongues will not be understood by
the gods.

Their time, and now is the time, has come.
[*To Ngam*]
Since when did you join their club?

Ngam
I am not an elder and I do not envy them or want to join them.

Bangsibu
In plain language, what is wrong in the world of the living?

Ngam
It is a man and his daughter.

Bangsibu
What has happened to them?

Ngam
Suicide.

Bangsibu
Suicide is good.

Ngam
There you go again, playing.

Bangsibu
I am not playing. I am just marvelled by your tale.
I am just examining the possibilities of your tale.
The greatness of this tale and how it will be told,
For a long time to come, to both the young and the old.
A man and the daughter! Suicide! That is an interesting tale.

Ngam
It is the Fuli Princess and her father. [*Disappointed.*]

Bangsibu

Where are they?

Ngam

Dead. Suicide. Gone for good.

Bangsibu

(*Looks at the ground,
Recites some incantations and
Pours libation again from his cup.*)

The will of the gods must always come to pass.
Blessed are those who understand it and obey.

Ngam

Are the gods aware of this disgrace?

Bangsibu

They willed it.

Ngam

Why should they do a thing like that?
At least Fuli was a great man and heir to the palace of Kom
And his daughter, a worthy Princess.

Bangsibu

I thought you asked a question?
But again, you give answers.
And yet, I must give you the right answers; the truth.
Listen.

(*Quick change of scene*)

Scene I

Light
At the palace of the chief of Fuli
Enter Tufoin and Yuh; all attendants.

Yuh

It seems to me that the moon of the village has found her sun.

Tufoin

The Prince of Belo,
The one to pay for the golden prize.

Yuh

Then he must be very lucky.
The moon of this village shines.
She shines in deeds.
She shines in thought and in words she shines.

Tufoin

I see you have changed from an attendant to a griot.

Yuh

How do you make the difference?

Tufoin

The attendant is quiet,
Because he knows the truth that bites.
He is quiet because his words can spill blood.
He is quiet because his tongue reveals not peace.
But, the griot is noisy,
He is noisy because he wants to eat.
He is noisy because he knows not what he sings.

Yuh

I am griot and you are attendant.

Is that what should make the heir of Belo unhappy about his bride in the person of our most exquisite moon?

Tufoin

I have not said so. I think the prince of Belo too is a worthy man.

Yuh

That makes the two of them better then.

Tufoin

It is their business.

The woman who does not eat the gizzard

Has nothing to say about the taste,

Even though she is the one who prepares it to be eaten.

Yuh

I have been wondering why Belo has been visiting Fuli

So much these past days. His son is lucky.

Tufoin

You had better caution her for I see your moon in clouds.

And the darkness to come that will spread through the land.

And you and I and all will be causalities.

And the moon will not shine.

And pain will reside in the land because of her doom.

Caution her before that time comes. Caution her great griot.

Yuh

You must be jealous of the Prince of Belo.

Be careful critical attendant.

Tufoin

Why?

Yuh

Because from your words, you surely are eyeing the noble Princess but you are too cowardly to face her. [*Laughs*]

Tufoin

I do not think so.
A termite can be eaten by any bird that wants to.

Yuh

There you lie.

Tufoin

Why?

Yuh [*Laughs.*]

I see I am right. You do not know your place. You should not have dreamed for this lady. She is not for you. She is for the prince.

Tufoin

Then who am I?

Yuh

You are a slave, by birth and upbringing. You are doomed to serve your master until this wretched life of yours ends in this troubled world of Fuli.

Tufoin

Who are the prince and princess?

Yuh

They are nobles by birth. They have their world which is not yours.

Tufoin

Do you know that someone is playing the drum already?

Yuh

If it is the prince, fine.
Any other person will be hastening his journey to *Sowe*;
There to meet his ancestors.

Tufoin

Fointama, our great hunter is coming. [*Enter Fointama.*]

Fointama

Is the morning good?

Yuh

Yes, our great hunter. It is good.

Tufoin

Are your boys also good?

Fointama

They are.
Just that hunting is becoming very difficult these days.

Yuh

We know that and we pray the gods for you.
You know we are confident about your team
And so, trust that you are up to the task for we have never
Lacked meat.

Tufoin

He that gives you good things is never forgotten
And forever is respected.
From the hills of Boyo to Bingo.
The great rivers of Mughom to the great palace at Laikom
Your name is praised for your mighty exploits.

---

[1] In Kom mythology, Sowe is the main passage that separates the world of the living and that of the dead.

Fointama

Thank you very much.
I must now go on to what I came for.
Is the moon of Fuli in her hut?
She summoned my presence.

Yuh

Great hunter, Hunter of all creatures,
She is there. But you must be careful.
When a master wants to eliminate his slave,
He makes him feel he is an equal.

Fointama

I am still a youth and hot in my blood.
Wise words are by me still incomprehensively understood.
Would wise palace dwellers make your proposal clear to me?
You know I only talk with the lions, leopards, tigers and rat
moles.

Tufoin

In plain words,
We mean that a goat has never beaten the lion in a jungle
court.
And if you must know, we are in a jungle.
Your life with lions and tigers is a better one.

Fointama

I will apply to this schooling but first let me see her royal
princess. [*Exit Fointama.*]

Tufoin

I tell you in truth, that is the prince of Belo's rival.

Yuh

You must be joking! [*Laughs loud and long*] Critical attendant
sir,
 That can't be. [*Laughs*]

9

A hunter? She will dismiss him like a cur.

Tufoin

In our own jungle,
He who has power is lion
And the lion cannot dismiss but help the cur to come to him.

Yuh

And what happens to the cur?

Tufoin

It panics as usual with its tail between its legs.
More than that, it cries. [*Laughs out loud and claps his hands*]

Yuh

How then does the beautiful one see the prince?

Tufoin

Griot investigator, she sees him as a bore;
As an impostor coming to disturb her love;
As a detractor who does not know where to belong.

Yuh

I see a boiling pot in this village.
I see dark clouds descending from Boyo.
I see the wrath of the gods.
I smell danger and famine and death.

Tufoin

Are you now tuned to my reason?
They that live in a jungle, as jungle men cannot be frightened
so easily.
Great palace griot, there is a song for you to sing.
To warn and not to praise is a supreme task.
May be the griot will be the one to change the jungle.
[*Exit Tufoin and Yuh.*]

10

Scene II

Still at Fuli
The princess's chamber
The princess is sitting with Ndum her maid.
They are having a serious discussion.

Ndum
My noble lady, on the day of your wedding, I shall adorn you with the best of hair styles. One that none in the tribe has ever had.

Princess
Ndum, don't you think you dream a lot for me? OK. Where did you see this style?

Ndum
I saw it in the Nsaw land when the noble queen of the village and I went to visit the Fon of the country of the Nsaw people.

Princess
And you kept it only to reveal it on my wedding day.
Why don't you give me a better one now before my great hunter;
This great one who has stolen my heart.
This mighty skilful one who comes into my presence?

Ndum
Is the prince coming?

Princess
Who is the prince? I am talking of my love who comes to enter into my arms.

11

Who is bolder than the lion
Who can move up and down Boyo for days without food and drink
Who has gone to *Sowe* many times yet is alive.

Ndum

And it is not the prince?

Princess

Ndum, I feel his footsteps.
I want to be alone now.

Ndum

Your orders, my royal princess, I will obey. [*Exit Ndum.*]

Fointama comes in
Observes the place like the Fon's guard.
Then, with a determined walk,
Moves towards the princess's chamber.
He by-passes Ndum,
They pause and stare at each other.
No one talks
And then, each continues in the opposite direction.
The hunter enters the chamber.

Princess

Yes great hunter.
There you come not at my request, but for love
And my love to you I will give all my days on earth. You come not by my orders
For the hunter of tigers will not be moved by such orders.
But the force of love has brought you here.

She moves towards Fointama.
Holds him on the shoulders and
Fointama is surprised

Fointama

Woman! Take care.
Are you kidding?

Princess

I am not kidding
Your love to me is pleasant like palm oil.
It is as pure as camwood.
Your name pierces into my body like a two edged cutlass.

Fointama

Woman! What you are trying to do is an offence to the tribe.
I will not engage myself in this race because I cannot win it.
So, let me go.

Princess

A bold hunter,
Yet with liver for a heart.
A leader, who knows not his powers…

Fointama

A leader who knows his place
In the forest.
A leader who gets in a natural jungle to feed the tamed jungle.
A leader who knows his power is not to touch a mother
tigress.
A leader who knows he is a goat and remains a goat.

Princess

You cannot be a victim.
You are as strong as the lion,
Greatest of our hunters, the griots sing your name,
For you feed the whole world.
You are faster than the deer
No wonder maidens love you.

[Bows her head
Prayer- like]

Oh gods of my father,
Help that I enter into the hut of this one,
And feel his manhood deep in my womanhood.
Great is Fointama.
Fointama whom the world fears,
Whose presence makes the jungle to tremble.
Who sets the lion on its heels.

[To Fointama]
 You cannot be a victim.
Come let me feel your warmth, mighty man.
Let me feel your warmth the greatest of this age.
Come, come and never depart.
Bless me. Hug me and clasp me with your strong arms. *[She
feels his biceps]*

Fointama

No, my princess, you are taboo
And bestowed to a great man.
I am just a servant. Doomed to fetch for a jungle and
To serve this race of privileged people.

Princess

Taboo am I,
Yet lovely and loving.
Do not turn me down great hunter, simply because
I am noble and you are a slave.
Love makes us one and united and enhances our dream of
respite for mankind.
Your presence by my side is like the aroma of a pleasant fruit.

Fointama

No! I fear for your future

Can I go now?

Princess

No don't go.

Fointama

Let me go
[Wriggles himself and runs out]

Princess

No! no! no!

She starts sobbing.
Enter the Prince of Belo.

Ayeah

Beautiful one, here I come.
You, who are as smooth as palm oil.
You, who are sweet, like fresh corn.
You, whom the world of men looks at with awe.
What puts you in this mood?
I, your love, am there to grant you comfort.

Princess

He is gone. *[Sobs the more.]*

Ayeah

Who is gone?

Princess

Gone for good
Into the jungle and my heart bleeds for him.

Ayeah

But I am here.
And I promise to love you

In good and bad weather.

Princess

But I do not love you.
[Sobs.] He is gone into the jungle.
He loves the jungle more than me.
He loves to feed on the untamed jungle
Yet, he hates me.

Ayeah

[Furious.] Who do you love?

Princess

[Still sobbing.] My heart will split.
He is gone into the jungle.
The one I love and the one I hate hangs around me….

Ayeah

[Shouts.] Stop! Stop! Stop!
Enough of this nonsense
If you must remember, you are betrothed to me as wife
And I am not going to let you go for any jungle-goer.

Princess

Who are you?

Ayeah

Good question, jungle princess and the jungle lover.
You forget too soon. That is part of jungle life.
You want to know who I am. Right?
I am a citizen of the jungle.
And in the jungle anything goes.

Rushes at her and in their struggle she falls to the ground.
Lights fade out.
Swift change of stage is noticeable when lights return
Still in the same chamber

The princess looks hurt, sad and calm.
The prince is apologetic from his looks.

Ayeah

The gods of Kom
I am so sorry to have hurt you my dear.
Please dear, can you forgive me?
I know it is an offence in Fuli and Belo and in all of Kom,
It is an offence that can hasten me to *Sowe's* gate.

Princess

How I wish that were possible so I can have my freedom.

Ayeah

Please, help me let us frame a lie to this effect.

Princess

What? It is a taboo to lie in this tribe.

Ayeah

My princess, you have a noble heart of innocence.
Such a heart charms even that of the lion
If only he remains king of the jungle.

Princess

It is a taboo to tell lies in this whole tribe of Kom

Ayeah

Those are all laws made by man.
The elders built such laws for their profit.
And we, of the younger generation must not abide by them
To our discredit.
Just stick with me and we will change those laws.

Princess

No! No! No!

Fight for your defence alone.
My father and all of Fuli will see my swollen face
And I shall tell them the truth
Nothing but the whole truth.

Ayeah

Most beautiful, most noble princess
How can I comfort you to show my regrets?
For such monstrous acts from my hot hands,
Shall even my tears compensate the grief in my heart?
But I know you are noble and by this great nobility of
Yours shall be at my defence.
For the hand that touches a noble princess of Kom
With such aggression and inhumanity must pay with his head.
And I swear with the name of my fathers and the gods at
Boyo
To do all you shall require should you stand by me and
protect
Me from the great wrath of the whole land.

Princess

[*Aside*] I thank the gods at Boyo for such great deliverance
From the bondage of such monstrous relationships that I
Never ever endorsed.
This proceeds from elders greed and for which the youth
Become victims. The gods at Boyo
Are always right by my fate,
I see Fointama, the one I love, about and around me. And
away with this monster,
Bestowed by the greed of ancient culture
For the pleasure of the past and the elders,
As a burden by my side and a constant pest.
[*To Prince*] If you accept never to come by me
For assistance, for my support or anything that
Requires two people to meet,
Then I shall stand by you in your defence.

Ayeah

Let it be so my Princess.
So what will you say?

Princess

I will tell a lie.
That means I will die.

Ayeah

You will not die.
You and I will disprove the old lie
Our fathers used to deceive the young
And when it is done a new song will be sung
And you and I will be great names in this tribe
And our deeds will be the subject of discussion for everyone
in the tribe
And our fame will grow tall
For our great deeds will never fall.
Daughter of the gods that master virtue and cunning
What lie has your guiding ancestor injected into your mind
For it shall grant me pleasure to listen to it.

Princess

Nothing yet.
[*Not looking at him.*]
Just go and I will think about it and you will know about it
first thing in the morning.

Ayeah

I will go with your noble words.
[*He leaves with his head down. Change of scene*]

Scene III

Belo chief's Palace. In the chamber of Prince Ayeah

Ayeah
This is a good opportunity for me
To outwit this unpleasant rival of mine.
For what has been rumoured to my hearing
I have come to hear and see it.
She is in love with him, [*Moves up and down the stage restless.*]
This cannot be true.
And in this relationship I am out of the way.
Therefore, the gods of this land must help me,
They must …and now
To out-play this enemy.
    [*pensively.*]
He is a great hunter and the dream of every woman
[*Agitated*]
And she that was betrothed to me,
And she that I so much love,
Has gone head and feet to him.
No!...No!... No!
I must fight him like a man
Full of wit.
[*Moves round the chamber aggressively to the rhythm of the
Njong music that is played is heard from far off.
The sound of cutlasses clash as the music reaches a crescendo and then
fades.*]
What is happening to me? I look heartbroken and weary in
my spirit.
Am I no longer the strong man?
My head is coming out of my body. [*Hits his fore head violently.*]
[*Enter Tosam.*]
I must fight this great hunter

For it is when you face the lion that you know your strength.
I should be able to tell all of Kom
And beyond that I am no coward.

Tosam
What makes you, noble Prince, to talk alone
In a lonesome hall?

Ayeah
Not much of a palaver. Just that a man must at one point suffer some anxieties.

Tosam
Anxiety. Did I hear you well my Prince?

Ayeah
Sure you did. Anxiety.

Tosam
When did the chick start to ponder about its food?
When did the trees start to cry out loud for lack of water or sunshine?
If the tree by the river side fears the drought what will the tree on the hill top do?
My Prince is anxious.
Shall the prince, most honoured and most privileged
Make a mockery of the other youths like him.
How can the owner of the land be anxious?
About what? Food, dress, wife or what?

Ayeah
Tosam you are not just a friend but more so like my brother.

Tosam
Yes I am.

Ayeah

I have never kept a secret from you. [*Fetches some drinks which he pours into two cups. Gives Tosam's a cup.*]

Tosam

You have never. [*Drinks from the cup.*]Good corn beer.

Ayeah

You are a man with a sharp brain that is sweet like salt.

Tosam

I am flattered. [*He says this bent over as a mark of respect*]

Ayeah

No, friend and brother, this is no time for flattery.
I am not singing an old love song for anybody.
For such songs are stale and do not necessarily
Stir the heart of the love one intends.

Tosam

Who have you flattered and failed?

Ayeah

None. But I am in a losing game.
Because you are my friend and brother with great wits
I employ you at my service
 to be my brain in this matter.

Tosam

I will do all for my Prince. What went wrong, where and how?

Ayeah

What went wrong, where and how?
I wish I could give you an answer
That is rich with the logic of the questions.

What would you say if you discover somebody's pestle pounding in another's mortar?

Tosam
Good riddle. Can you help interpret this wisdom?

Ayeah
No. Let me put it rightly now. What would you say when a cock comes close to eagles to eat and drink with them?

Tosam
The cock will be blind. It is not because they all have wings that the cock should think it can be an eagle.

Ayeah
You are a man of great wisdom and to you I lay my case.
You know my wife or wife to be….

Tosam
Eh...Yes my Prince.
The Princess of Fuli, your betrothed.

Ayeah
Your brain is sharp and has not been corrupted by corn beer.
She is in love with that Fointama,
 Head of the hunters of the tribe.
[*He falls silent. Tosam mouth hangs open in surprise. Then he covers it with his right palm*]
She even told me to my face that she loves him and I could not stand it,
In rage my hands fell upon her noble body and wounded her face.
 That is another problem.
As you know, the laws of Kom state that anyone who touches a woman will be punished and when this woman is a princess he must suffer violent death.

Tosam

My Prince. My prince. What irrational acts from your noble hands and mind?

Ayeah

I hastened to ask her what she would ask of me if she must conceal me.

She, immediately, said she would want me out of her sight forever.

Tosam

Another irrational thought…

Ayeah

From a desperate mind! Then I agreed with her and asked her what lie she will frame to save my soul. For which she said she knows nothing yet; that before the morning gets old tomorrow she will reveal it to me.

Tosam

Pray the gods that she has no idea.

Ayeah

What? That will mean reporting me.

Tosam

Does the hunter know what he is up to?

Ayeah

Hunter or no hunter, my life is at stake
My angry hands fell on the princess
And Kom cannot accept that for the law is straight.

Tosam

The law?

Ayeah

The law

Tosam

Says who?

Ayeah

The law is the law!

Tosam

My prince. You make me ponder if you know who you are.
You grumble and panic like a goat and not a tiger.

Ayeah

I panic and grumble like a goat and not a tiger?

Tosam

If you do not know who you are,
Know that the law's hands can be tied
Even to make the tiger right when it is wrong.

Ayeah

[*Looks at Tosam. Tosam looks at Ayeah*]
Know that the law's hands can be tied
Even to make the tiger right when it is wrong.

Tosam

As your royal tongue did confess
She promises to protect you if you must never come near her.

Ayeah

If I must never come near her
I am saved.

Tosam

And you are set never to go near her?

Ayeah

For my life's sake.

Tosam

And what if the great hunter is no more?

Ayeah

A wild dream of course!

Tosam

There you are. If she will not want of you and will protect you, pray Boyo that nothing comes out of her feeble womanly brain and then you shall propose that she accuse the hunter as the tormenter of her flesh. For this cause, if she agrees, then my Prince shall save his life and have his Princess.

Ayeah

[Surprised. He smiles. He carries Tosam. Puts him down and they both sing a song of victory and dance. The drums, the gong, the rattle and the horn all accompany this warrior song.]
You are a great brain.
A brain to consult in times of trouble,
A brain that is faster than the flash of lightening,
And a man worthy of trust.
Tosam? Tosam Tosam? You are a wise man. I bless the day I knew you.

Tosam

My duty is to make my Prince happy.

Ayeah

Even if she has an idea, I will push this one down her throat. After all she is woman and woman is soft, weak and foolish. I am not the one who says it. It is seen.

Tosam

Just be careful not to tell her that she is soft, weak and foolish because then you will discover that women are strong, tough and intelligent.

Ayeah

Trust me. I will plead and even worship her and make sure she hears and agrees with me.

I thank you so much. Let us drink more of this beer to celebrate our victory.

[*The music off stage continues and they sing and dance in warrior fashion.*

Exit]

Scene IV

At the palace of the chief of Fuli
Enter Tufoin and Yuh

Tufoin

Have you heard the news?

Yuh

That Fointama slapped the beautiful one?

Tufoin

Yes.

Yuh

It's terrible. These young men are too hot.
Our elders say, and rightly too that a hot body ends only in trouble.

Tufoin

Are you sure he did it?

Yuh

You think that story is a lie?

Tufoin

Fointama cannot do that. A man who cries in front of a woman will not have the guts to clout her.

Yuh

A man who cries in front of the woman is the boldest man in the land.
A man who cries in front of the woman is capable of bringing tigers

And meat of all sorts from the jungle for us as food.
That is no shy person.

Tufoin

You are right.
From the common sense point of view,
Every finger will point at Fointama.

Yuh

Why will the noble princess, in her royalty, accuse him of all men?

Tufoin

Why will she accuse him? As a woman's way to fight back may be.

Yuh

Nobles don't lie in Kom. It is a princess we are talking about here.

Tufoin

Why does she accuse Fointama?
In the jungle, anything goes.

Yuh

Of course! A hunter comes to a chief's palace,
Beats a princess
And goes to the jungle free.
Then, men and women are left to debate on it.
Oh Yuh Fukuyn, the great Fon of Kom, what is happening to your land and laws?

Tufoin

From common sense, everyone will reason and lament like you.
But, a deeper thought will reveal the truth

Of this jungle.

Yuh

Critical attendant. Keep thinking.
The facts are clear and should be handled.

Tufoin

I put one and one together.
I see Fointama a victim;
I see the princess a bigger victim.
But, this scheme is still beyond my revelation.

Yuh

Ok. We wait and see what comes out.

Tufoin

We wait, look and dig into this matter.
[Exit.]
Enter Ngoh and Ntam on the other side of the stage.
The setting should shift to demonstrate an early evening scene.
*The crickets are singing in a clear moon night. The bright moon
penetrates their hut.*
*Sounds of drums and ululations are heard from far off. They are roasting
cocoyams, the evening delicacy.*

Ntam

Have you heard the news from the village?

Ngoh

Yes. Someone told me that our leader, Fointama, slapped the
beautiful princess of Fuli.
*[In silence, they inspect cocoyams, scrub off the burnt parts and place
them back in fire]*

Ntam

I guess he must have been so offended to take that extreme step.

That young man has never smashed an insect knowingly.

Ngoh

He cannot hurt an insect knowingly.

He can hurt the Princess knowingly. [*Heaves a mocking sigh*]

Ntam

What do you mean by that?

[*Ngoh picks his cocoyam again, scrubs it as before and puts it back among the red coals*]

I hope Ngoh you are not up to something oh?

Ngoh

Just take a good look at yourself.

[*Mimicks*] I hope you are not up to something oh.

Like a child born yesterday. I am up to something.

Now listen.

I thank the gods of Boyo for this thing. That Fointama must die.

[*Ntam looks at him expressing some shock at his pronouncement.*]

Ntam

Eh…ma,

Ngoh, be careful, jealousy is what kills a man.

Ngoh

This is not about jealousy. It is about the youth taking up offices of responsibility and we the elderly being asked to serve under our very children.

Ntam

And the solution is to eat up the children, is that it?

Ngoh

Take it to mean whatever thing. But here is the jungle and here he who is fastest gets the booty. That youth played his game and was given to lead us. [*Waves his head in disapproval.*] Me… Ngoh… Hunter of Kom for many years yet always second in command even to my children.

Ntam

But that should not be reason enough to hate a loving and duty-conscious young man.
As far as I am concerned, the gods in Boyo and the demons of the red soil can bear me witness that this boy, though a child, is one of the greatest hunters and leaders in Kom.

Ngoh

Says who?

Ntam

Says me.

Ngoh

You are naïve. The hair of wisdom mourns on your head.

Ntam

The greatest of wisdom is seen when one is honest to acknowledge greatness.

Ngoh

Then in your wisdom, what kind of eternal assistant is me?

Ntam

You can be a noble one but not when your mind is so corrupt.

Ngoh

You are naïve. In the jungle only the corrupt must survive,

The honest and innocent die and rot unnoticed,
They are destroyed. The Hawks fetch not only the unjust but most especially the just.
It pays to understand the jungle and be like the jungle being.

Ntam

And how do you get to that?

Ntam

Simple. The hyena does not hunt but eats good meat because he is a friend to the lion.
In that case, the hyena is wise and knows how to play the game of survival.

Ntam

You speak with a witty and crafty tongue. How long did you listen to the voice of elders?

Ngoh

That is not much of a matter.
As the sun moves from one part of the sky
To the other, so too must our minds, our dreams and our goals move.
Do you agree?

Ntam

Agreed.

Ngoh

Then you are a wise man.

Ntam

But…

Ngoh

No buts here. Get this. This opportunity is not to waste. I assist Fointama and you assist me. He is a great hunter no doubt. [*Pauses*] But who cares in the jungle? We are both elderly and he is a youth. That means the two of us need to get him out of the way. See the way the whole tribe of Kom worships this youth. I hope you will love to be like that. [*Pause*] Ntam I want us to testify against Fointama in front of the village council so that they [*With gestures*] cut off his head, then you and I will be the lords of the forest.

Ntam
[*The drums are heard faintly off stage. The music has a melancholic tone*]
So they are beating all of these drums that Nteff is truly gone.

Ngoh
Dead and gone!

Ntam
And his seasons in ruins!

Ngoh
And his seasons in ruins!

Ntam
Without wife and child anymore!

Ngoh
Without wife and child anymore [*Pause*] But you see what I tell you.
 We have wives and children and also grandchildren like Fointama our lord. Yet they are made to lead us. It is a pity. [*Silence*] As to my suggestion, what is your opinion on that?

Ntam
Ngoh. I am not there.

35

That is murder.

Ngoh

No. A means to survive.

Ntam

But what is so special in that girl and her likes that when slapped, it becomes an issue of life and death?

Ngoh

Your philosophy has no place here.
In the jungle, the question is how we profit from the event.
After all it is dishonourable for a man so appreciated to be smacking girls.

Ntam

But my mind tells me he did not.

Ngoh

Ntam's mind is not Kom's mind.

Ntam

We need to hone our consciences.

Ngoh

Our consciences you say!. In this land, conscience died even before Yuh Fukuyn became the leader and created Afo-a-Kom.

Ntam

If the gods that reside at Boyo
Cannot be corrupted and their wisdom,
If they stand as the divine judges to our land
Then shall I swear in and by their names never to be a conspirator.
To your game, Ngoh, my spirit rejects and having eaten all my coco yams
I will take my leave to sleep.

[Exists. The Njang is still heard playing faintly.
Sound of crickets
And the moon too lights up the world. The same hut
Ngoh sitting in the same position]

Ngoh

To work with cowards is a crime.
I am determined to win the position of head hunter
And to the gods and demons of this land
(Which ever organized such scheme) I give thanks.
I'd planned to poison the youth
And now, my poison shall be my tongue.
Ngoh. Fortune awaits you. You must have it, so
Farewell Fointama.
[Exit.]

Scene V

The Princess's chamber at Fuli
She is sitting down
Neatly and royally dressed.
She is very composed and relaxed.
But it is obvious from her facial appearance that she has come up dry.
She hits her fore head.
Then the Prince of Belo comes in.

Ayeah

Is the morning good?

Princess

Is this where you come to find out whether your morning is good?

Ayeah

No noble one. I am here for peace.
For my mind has lots of battles;
Battles of endless ages since my rage
Pushed me into exercising my irrational freedom.
I am for peace
That we may agree upon your discourse that will
Free me from the laws of this land.
I am for peace
And I stand at your mercy; might and understanding
That will restore my place. Please may your noble voice speak
kind words to this disparate soul;
Tormented by its own acts; tormented by its desire to express
love and alas! Some stupid action as the Tribe will think and
say and judge.
I am for peace
And I come for peace.

Princess

I understand. I will and am ready to keep my part of the bargain. But I am not able to conceive a lie. You know as I do that it is a difficult and expensive art. I will need to train myself for a while to the exercise.

Ayeah

[*To himself*] You are noble but naïve. Ever since the gods climbed into the uppermost part of Boyo, nobility has resided in deceit and the ability to deal with a strong enemy and usurp his place.
[*To the Princess*] That issue is partly solved. If you shall agree to make rumour true. This is a jungle.

Princess

And what rumours are going on?

Ayeah

The Princess was slapped.

Princess

What?

Ayeah

The Princess was slapped.

Princess

How did they know?

Ayeah

The jungle has its roles and every tale and play is revealed even without substance. The rumour continues that she was slapped by the hunter Fointama.

Princess

It is not true. You did this.

Ayeah

That will mean hurting you the more. That will mean digging my grave deeper. I have no hand in this rumour. But I think it is a good opportunity for me if you apply to this rumour.

Princess

Then Fointama will be killed.

Ayeah

No one, not even the Fon of Kom can dare to request his death.
He is the greatest of our hunters.
Kom respects him and will do all to save his soul.
Even you will fight for his rescue later.
Just apply to this rumour to see my soul freed from the battles and dreams of *Sowe*.

Princess

Then I shall tell my father the rumour is true and when the game is over, you shall never come my way.

Ayeah

That is the deal.
[Exit.]

Scene VI

The palace court at Fuli
Enter the chief of Belo, the chief of Fuli. Hunters, maids, the Prince of
Belo and the Princess of Fuli.
They all sit at their usual traditional positions.
The four village judges come in and take their seats.
The sharer of Njong takes his place and the different individuals
Bow to the ikeng for their cups to be filled with corn beer.
Then the chief of Fuli stands and clears his throat.

Fuli

Ooooh Kom.
What is the subject for our gathering here today?
[*Fointama is brought in. He is tied with ropes. He is pushed down to sit.*]
Whenever we gather here, we know it is no good news for somebody. What good is there to meet just to separate again, leaving someone sad and another happy? This affects us too. Can the eye be in pain and the ear smiles? The land of Kom, as the Fon, our great ruler, hates such meetings. I, his faithful subject and leader of Fuli, think same. We have asked and pleaded to no avail that people should help us not to come here. Since people like us to be here, we too must never stop to come. [*Pauses*] Today's case is suicidal. [*Turns to his daughter*] Look at her, my daughter.[*Hits his chest. Waves his hand. Then to Fointama, wags his finger*] My daughter, beaten in Fuli, in my palace, by a slave of a hunter. I rest my case because I know that we are benevolent people and have laws to guide and protect us.

Belo

We say the body that is hot like a pot on fire ends in trouble.
We also say over-excitement is dangerous

And such danger subjects the land of Kom to shame
And a mark of scorn to her name.
The gods of this land honour us and our name
And in justice we have saved this fame
Since Tang Na Koli led the journey from the plain.
This act; beating a Princess of Fuli, daughter of the heir
Of Kom, is sacrilegious and to me,
Father in-law to be of this noble lady, who by the gods was betrothed
To my son. If Kom be cowards and forfeit the law,
Then we are in trouble. For Fointama is great.
Fointama feeds us more than any hunter,
But the law is greater than us all.
Until the Fon of Kom in his royal wisdom implores us otherwise.
We do not live in a jungle. We are noble people and should act as such.
[*To Fuli*.]I hope I have spoken well my brother.

Fuli

You have spoken well and wisely. As a land of law, the proceedings of this court must be open and we implore all to speak in freedom and justice that guides this great land. With this, we will all be free from the wrath of the gods when justice will be meted on the culprit.

Ayeah

My fathers, I greet you all.
The noble Princess there seated and I were bound together by the gods.
This bonding is so strong that in my heart I can feel her state of mind.
On that fateful day, I sat in my chamber worried about her
And my spirit tortured me to go for her rescue;
If I am a man of vigour and might in a land where might pays.

44

I succumbed to the challenge of my spirit and out
Of my chambers and alone, I ran as fast as I could.
To rescue her, that is, my to be wife.
[*Shakes his head in disappointment*]
[*In cold melancholic voice.*]I was late.[*Pause.*] Very very late.
The gloom on her face was great.
Her agony was bitter and pierced my marrow.
I sought to know why she was in this state and ready to kill.
[*Draws his cutlass*]
Just to be told that [*Pointing to Fointama*]this wretched slave
committed the offence. He stole himself into her chambers,
and beat her for want of love.

Malayena
My noble Princess, is this true what we hear happened to you.

Princess
[*Panics*] Yes yes yes

Malayena
Take heart. We will protect you as the law demands.

Ayeah
She is still shocked by the barbaric jungle act.

Malayena
[*Looks at her.*] With whom were you in your chamber?

Princess
I was with Ndum, my maid. She was braiding my hair.

Malayena
My lords, the Princess is still in shock. Let me speak with
Ndum who was with her.
[*Ndum comes in and stands at the centre stage*]

Our daughter, you look smart today. I hope you understand why you are here. Tell us the truth about what you saw and how this terrible offence came to be.

Ndum

I was with the Princess and was braiding her hair. She was waiting for the Prince of Belo, her love as she will call him and sing songs to praise him and dance for him. Suddenly, the hunter, Fointama broke in and forced his way into the chamber. His eyes were wild like the angry and hungry lion behind a desperate antelope. I was ordered out by his roaring voice and after some time, I heard her weep in great pain.

Ajimsibom

Did you see any other person enter the house after the hunter?

Ndum

I did not.

Ajimsibom

And what did you do when you heard her cry as you say?

Ndum

I went to the chamber and there, as the gods will have it, the hunter was gone and the noble Prince was there to comfort her of her pain.

Malayena

So you say you did not see the hunter come out and the Prince come in.

Ndum

I did not.

Abembom

It means there are many entrances into the Princess's chamber.

And in this dark, what then do you think happened to the Princess?

Ndum

When I looked at the eyes of Fointama, I feared for the Princess and Fuli. I am convinced his great rage caused him to do such cruelty on a noble one.

Malayena

Now, Princess of Fuli, could you kindly tell this village who Fointama is to you and how he found himself in your guarded chamber.

Princess

I admire him for his skill at hunting.

I sense the lions and tigers and leopards trembling at his feet.

I regard him as the greatest and the boldest of Kom at all times.

But,

[*She shakes her head*]

He went too far.

He will steal time in the forest;

He will enter the yard in great secret and will tell me all the tales of jungle life;

Tales of love and sweet ones of course. I must say, he tells me all the things I like

As no man in this land ever could make woman feel.

His soft but manly voice, his caring and soothing caresses and great smile made me happier

And I longed to remain with him.

I admire him for who he is.

[*Then shakes her head again.*]

47

This act, he committed when I tried to stop him from getting into me.

All

Eeeeeeeeeeeeh

Ntam

That is an abomination in all of Kom.

Abembom

Did the hunter know you had such strong admiration for him?

Princess

To speak the truth, he knew because I have said so to him.

Abembom

Did he ever force himself into you?

Princess

No. Not at all! Only on that day.

Ayeah

I hoped and prayed to meet him, then I would have forced him to vomit okro. Carved thing.

Abembom

My noble men of Kom, what we gather from this is that there is something going on between Fointama and the Princess and this thing is spearheaded by the Princess. Fointama, do you have anything to say?

Fointma

[Sitting in ropes tied around his hands and feet
He speaks without lifting his head. Bowed to the earth.]
Noble men of Kom, I am in a dream land. Things are turning so fast and so unreal. I do not understand where I am. I do

not understand anything. I do not understand any word. I do not understand myself.

Ajimsimbom
You seem not to understand. This means you are guilty of the act.

Abembom
Fointama. You must be a man and say something. Defend yourself. What is your response to what the women said? Speak!

Fointama
Those women. [*Without lifting his head*] They are real tortoises that are possessed by the demon of tricks and lies on earth.

Malayena
So Fointama, owner of all truth, tell us the truth and do not insult people as liars. [*Pauses*] Is there any testimony to this case?

Ngoh
Yes. [*He moves to the centre stage*] I have some things to say as regards the issue at stake and the involvement of my boss the great hunter, Fointama.

Malayena
You were with Fointama?

Ngoh
I am with Fointama.

Maleyena
You are his assistant?

Ngoh

I am his assistant.

Maleyena

You people hunt night and day?

Ngoh

We hunted night and day.

Maleyena

You hunted night and day. What is that supposed to mean?

Ngoh

When I heard this story, it did not surprise me. If you notice well you will realize that our meat to the land has reduced. It is because Fointama was in love. Each time he sits, it is the name of the Princess he calls, he sings of that name from the time the sun says good morning to when it says good bye for the day.

Maleyena

And what has that to do with beating the Princess?

Ngoh

On that day, Fointama was acting strange. He was wrathful. He called the name of the Princess and then the Prince and swore to Boyo and the red soil. His muscles were strong. We feared and could not stop him. He called the name of the Princess and roared as he left the forest in rage.

Maleyena

So you are sure he did it?

Ngoh

The way he left. Anything could have happened.

Ajimsimbom
Are you by that confirming that he did it?

Ngoh
I am confirming that he could do it.

Abembom
Ngoh, tell us, what is the name of the Princess.

Ngoh
In his great wrath he mentioned the title Princess, some other names that I have never heard. Maybe anger made him creative in names.

Abembom
This man is an unfortunate liar. You are a crafty creator of all that is evil. My fellow judges, Fointama had no interest in the Princess and so his innocence to these charges against him can be justified.

Fuli
This case is taking too long and leading us nowhere. The only person who can speak the truth here is the victim. My daughter, tell us who victimized you and this case is over.

Princess
Fointama.
There is grumbling in the court room.
A mark of approval and disapproval
People begin to rise and are threatening to leave

Abembom
It is a lie. Fointama is innocent. May I make one request? This case seems to have the gods in active force and I suggest we get to the oracle to reveal the truth to us.

Belo

Bobe Abembom has spoken rightly. Let Bangsibu, the eye of the gods report here as soon as possible before the next session.

[Exit]

Scene VII

At Fuli
Enter Yuh and Tufoin

Tufoin
It's useless sitting here all afternoon. Let us go down to the corners and have some corn beer. .
[Yuh looks at Tufoin and Tufoin looks at him.]

Yuh
Did you say leave? You are not serious. Don't you know this case is important to us? I tell you I cannot miss a second of the things that are happening here.

Tufoin
Can't we allow every ganakoh to carry his cattle stick? What is interesting in this case for you? The jungle says you and I are slaves. The jungle says they are nobles. Two people, two worlds, two destinies yet one Kom, one tribe and one place.

Yuh
I understand your philosophy my brother. But you still do not understand. We are slaves. Call us – you and I dog. But we are not underdogs. And this land is made up of underdogs. In front of underdogs, dogs are lords. Tomorrow, yes tomorrow, I will have enough to eat and drink because many underdogs will be interested to hear from me what the truth of the matter with jungle nobles is. You know what I will say. *[Beats his chest]* We took the right decision.

Tufoin
You are right. But that is where the problem is. What shall it benefit a people who eat and damn their land? When injustice

transforms a people to jungle beasts and food and drink govern their thinking, can the people ever reason? When people in jungle life scheme and kill for love and power, food and drink, will Mbom, the creator, rejoice or regret at his handiwork? Is this the great tribe of Kom?

Yuh
The problem with you is that you think and philosophize….

Tufoin
The problem is you, who is just a parrot passing for a griot. If you have to sing this farce of justice what shall be your song?

Yuh
Watch your mouth. Well, that once the great hunter over-stretched his confines and faced the law of the jungle.

Tufoin
No. That once upon a time, the lion looked for a goat to atone for its sins and the land of hungry griots sang a false tale.

Yuh
That seems true. But will the sin of the lion be atoned for?

Tufoin
I shall know if the gods are also drunk with wine and food only after Bangsibu must have come. Let us get into my hut.
[They move to the right stage
Get into Tufoin's hut
Sit.
Tufoin goes to a pot near a bed.
Takes the corn beer and pours it carefully into a calabash
Moves gently and bent forward.
He places it before them.]
This is corn beer brother. Drink and have peace.

Yuh

Drink and have peace.

Tufoin

Drink in honour of the jungle and its laws.

Yuh

Drink in honour of the jungle and its laws.

Tufoin

Drink that the underdogs shall never be dogs and nobles.

Yuh

The underdogs shall never be dogs and nobles. But this wine is beautiful and its taste is full in the mouth. Who prepared it?

Tufoin

My wife.

Yuh

Your wife is great.
I use to think that even the soil of the jungle is sour;
The reason for the poor corn
And therefore, poor beer.

Tufoin

My brother, you are right.
[*Mimics*]
Here we stand, in the name of the most high Fon of this land,
Protector and most wise of the land.
Chief of all the land's institutions, the invisible and omnipresent
Yet only wise leader of the land of law.
We do pay him our allegiance for his wisdom in checking and permitting that corn continues to grow and we continue to have beer to drink in peace.

Yuh

In peace?

Tufoin

In peace.
You have seen nothing yet. For peace there is.
A great achievement.
And peace protects the land
And it's above the dogs
And the likes of Fointama shall be victims of peace
And they that are hungry will not feed
For peace which the wisest ruler prescribes shall reign…

Yuh

Shut up. Shut up and shut up.
You are a servant and should protect this peace and not
throw words like little girls.

Tufoin

The words of a little girl are law;
And Fointama's fate is in such words.
[Exit]

Scene VIII

The palace court as in the previous scene
Two boys, strong and dripping with sweat walk across front stage.
They are followed by an old man in his worn out dala[2]
He uses his walking stick to guide his way.
He seems to be staggering for age seems to be heavy on him.
The two boys look behind. They want to beckon him,
But they show some sign of fear, an indication that it will be dangerous.
The old man walks gently to the centre stage.
Looks at the audience and shakes his head; a sign of pity.
The old man looks at Fointama,
Who remains seated, in ropes.
He shakes his head once more.
He removes from his aged ridden bag an old animal skin mat which he
Puts on the floor and then sits on it.

Bangsibu

I hear you want me. Here I am.

Belo

Old one. We salute you.

Bangsibu

I salute you. What is the cause of my summons here and today?

Belo

We understand that your wisdom surpasses that of ordinary mortals like us. The matter in front of us, we cannot satisfactorily handle it to please the gods until you come in to

---

[2] The Dala is a traditional male dress.

tell us the mind of the gods in this sacrilege that has come over us. The laws of the land state that no man touches a woman with the hand and that if that happens to a princess, the culprit will be put to death. What do you say to what has happened here at Fuli?

Bangsibu

[*Irritated*] So you cannot even handle crisis that concern you again?
You want to involve everybody in this rigmarole and your way of doing things.

Ajimsibom

Wise one, it is above us.

Bangsibu

Above you indeed;
It is above you because you have refused to take decisions.

Malayena

We have no decision…

Bangsibu

Yet the young man is tied and accused and you have no decision

Fuli

He is just a suspect. In areas where men are respected like ours, you are only a criminal when proven.

Bangsibu

[Looks into his bag.
He removes some cowries
And declares.]
I see the lion roaring at the panic of goats.

Yet in their escape, the lion gets one and a noble lion, it takes the goat to a court of lions.

Come what may, I see the goat is meat. And in lion court that can only be the fairest of judgments.

That is what I see and that is all.

I must warn you not to offend the gods in anyway.

Ajimsibom

Wise one, help us have justice.

Bangsibu

You know what is just. So apply it.

Are you not schooled in the rules of this land?

[He gets up,

Folds his things. Looks at them all and then leaves.]

Yuh

[Aside] Terrible things are about to happen and our priest has grown mad.

Fuli

We have received too much insult in this case. I am going to ask two questions and he who is accused will face the law.

Ajimsimbom

And we damn the consequences and the gods.

Malayena

Which gods? Do not mind the old man. He has become the child again. He babbles.

Abembom

Let me ask first…

Belo

No. We will hear nothing more from you. You are the cause of these insults.

Abembom

As a citizen of this land, I deserve to be listened to. What I say now is that we must be careful for the gods will fight us. [*Exits*]

Malayena

Go. We are ready for the gods. What is it? Gods. Gods. Gods.

Fuli

This is the question. My Princess and daughter, who touched you in this most brutal and animalistic way?

Princess

Fointama

Fuli

Tufoin did you people see Fointama enter her chamber?

Tufoin

Yes but er…er…er

Ajimsimbom

No more buts. The case is closed. The verdict is clear. The victim is undoubted.

Scene IX

Bare stage
A lamentation njang is produced from the back stage.
Fointama is led to the centre from the left stage by three Nikang masquerades.
His head is covered.
His hands are tied to his back.
Abembom comes in,
He whispers in the ear of Bobe-Aboh
Who affirms with a nod.

Bobe-Aboh

Wait a minute and unmask the criminal. *[Fointama is unmasked.]*

Abembom

Fointama,
Great hunter of Kom,
Is it the will of the gods
That you end as such?
I do not blame the gods for they have given us the ability to will,
To think and to act.

Fointama

But the gods ordained it.
That is why a slave must remain victim to his master.
Bobe, if the gods are just
May they reward you for fighting for me.

Abembom

I am a son of Kom
Of the tree of the Ikue

The tree of the Fons of Kom
Raised to enjoy the sweetness of justice.

Fointama

You are a stranger in this jungle. Your innocence as a lamb among tigers may put you in trouble.

Abembom

I have overcome fear and not even death will make me to forego the sweetness of justice.

Fointama

I am only a hunter.

Abembom

You are a man, created by Mbom;
Guided by Ikeng, Iwayn, and by Ifoyini;
The gods of Kom.
But one thing I ask of you. *[Pause]*
Let me hear your part of this story.
It shall be told to future generations.

Fointama

To speak the truth, I was her royal princess's guest on the day she was brutalized.

Abembom

[Surprised.] That means you had an affair with her?

Fointama

Not at all. But she wanted me to. On that fateful day, she sang to me her love songs. When I sensed she was getting hot like a bitch in heat, I broke loose from her and flew. I knew my place, I am a hunter. I knew she was for a prince. So my heart could not go for her.

Abembom

So she attacked you?

Fointama

She did not. I also cannot tell who attacked her for truly I saw no one enter her chamber after me. May be the gods did so as a means to call me to their bosom. I am glad to go. I will see my ancestors without fault; a pure man. That should be Fointama's song in all of Kom.

Bobe-Aboh

[Listening to the discussion shakes his head in pity. Then in a weak voice]
It is alright. We must do our job.

Fointama

I go as a hero. No one should lament for me. Lament for the land of Kom.
[Exit Fointama and others]

Abembom

Oh Kom, what is happening to you?
What is this disease that has attacked just the seedlings?
It has attacked the Fons
It has attacked the princes and princesses
It has attacked the chiefs
I am counting to leave who when the whole land is involved?
My brothers and sisters, I ponder,
And I have remained pondering.
[He sings a dirge and exits]

Scene X

[In the Princess's Chamber]

Princess

Could the world be so cruel to me? How can my struggle turn against me? Fointama! No you do not deserve to die! *[She weeps bitterly.]*
[Enter the chief of Fuli.]

Fuli

My dear Princess, what moves you to these endless tears? Your enemy has been eliminated. So rejoice noble one.

Princess

No. Bobo. He is not my enemy. He is a friend and the one I so love. Oh gods! What have I done to myself?

Fuli

Daughter. Did I hear you well?

Princess

You did father.
It was the prince that hit me.
I inclined to his scheme to free myself from the yoke of a loveless marriage.

Fuli

And it was Fointama you loved?

Princess

It is Fointama I love.

Fuli

Waaaaaaaaaaa ooooooooooooooo! Kom hear me. Do you mean that you caused the death of an innocent man?

Princess

Not for him to die was my plan.
But for me to go freely to his hut
Without tribal constraints to any prince.

Fuli

[Breathes deeply.
Looks at the ground
Walks towards his daughter.]
It is alright. Fointama must be dead by now. Stop crying and learn to start loving the prince.

Princess

I will not marry the prince. I have never loved him and will not betray Fointama anymore.

Fuli

But Fointama is dead.

Princess

Him alone will I marry in this world and beyond.

Fuli

My daughter, only make sure you do nothing funny.

Princess

I will do just what is noble.

Fuli

You are a true daughter of your father.
[Exits.]

Princess

My life is in shambles.
For my most noble betrayal of a man
Innocent, most loved and closed to my heart.
How can I atone for this sin if not with my blood?
Fointama, my effort was to have you
But you are gone.
I will give myself to no one.
I shall prove to Kom that I have my body and my being.
I have chosen you, Fointama, and you alone shall have me.
But, I have sent you to *Sowe's* gate in an unjust manner. I am coming to meet you.
Where you and I shall be in a land that knows no master and no servant.
Fointama,
I am coming.
[Exit]

Scene XI

At Fuli.
Enter Belo. He is received by Fuli as custom demands.

Belo
I hope all is well and our wife to be has recovered.

Fuli
Your wife to be is recovering.

Belo
The turn of things makes me think.

Fuli
The signs are bad.
The wind blows strong and the anus of the fowl is soon to be revealed.
My daughter says Fointama never touched her.

Belo
If that is true, then it is bad indeed.
Then we should proceed to bring the two children together soonest.
That may make the gods unable to act against us.

Fuli
You are right.
[Ndum enters. In great panic.]
What is wrong again.

Ndum
Bobo. The…the….the….princess.

Belo

What is wrong with her?

Ndum

Blood. Blood on her. Blood everywhere around her.
[They all rush off stage.
Same scene.
Re-enters Fuli with tears supported by Belo]

Belo

What boldness from a young woman?
To take her life with her own hands.

Fuli

I wish I could have stopped her.

Belo

I shall return to console my son before he too takes away his
life. *[Exit Belo.]*

Fuli

Farewell brother. Till we meet again after *Sowe.*
I am filled with guilt
For I could have protected her
And helped her walk according to her will.
She has taught me that humans are equal.
I loved her and now she is my teacher. In the shame of such
an event,
I must go after her. I must do this to atone for my sin against
Fointama and my daughter.
[Exit]

Epilogue

Still in the grove as in the prologue

Bangsibu
After my tale, what again shall you say son?

Ngam
Oh pity. Then, the prince of Belo is still alive,
I fear worse things may happen.
I hear the people say for injustice to stop, they need a
people's government and not blood government.

Bangsibu
They may have a point. Blood government can be good if
only man is respected and the gods and their values kept.

Ngam
When shall that happen?

Bangsibu
Now, and with you and me and others, each in their little
corner. Are you ready?

Ngam
I am.

[Exit.]